Cats in Fancy Glasses

A Whimsical Coloring Book for Cat Lovers

This book belong to

____

____

Preface

Welcome to the enchanting world of "Cats in Fancy Glasses," a delightful coloring book that celebrates the elegance and playfulness of our feline friends. Within these pages, you will embark on a captivating journey through a collection of cat portraits, each donning their own unique and stylish eyewear, all while being embraced by enchanting floral leaves and patterns.

As you immerse yourself in the artistic adventure of coloring, let your imagination roam free and bring these feline companions to life. From the regal Siamese sporting a pair of retro cat-eye glasses to the mischievous Maine Coon with colorful round spectacles, every cat breed is represented with its own distinctive charm. With each stroke of your coloring tool, you have the power to infuse personality and vibrancy into these whimsical feline faces.

The presence of floral leaves in the background and surrounding each cat serves as a reminder of the inherent connection between our feline companions and the natural world. Just as flowers bloom in vibrant hues, these cats express their individuality through their choice of fancy glasses, making each portrait a unique fusion of nature and style.

Whether you're an avid cat lover, an art enthusiast, or simply seeking a creative and relaxing escape, "Cats in Fancy Glasses" offers you a chance to unwind and find joy in the creative process. Get lost in the intricate details, from the delicate petal-like patterns to the intricate designs on the glasses, and watch as these charming feline personalities come alive under your artistic touch.

So, grab your favorite coloring tools and prepare to embark on a whimsical journey through the world of "Cats in Fancy Glasses." May this coloring book bring you moments of tranquility, inspiration, and a renewed appreciation for the beauty and individuality of our beloved feline companions. Happy coloring!

Cats: Our Fascinating and Beloved Companions

ntroduction:

Cats, known scientifically as Felis catus, are small, carnivorous mammals that have been cherished by humans for thousands of years. As one of the most popular pets worldwide, cats have captivated our hearts with their independent nature, charming personalities, and graceful movements. In this article, we will explore the remarkable characteristics and endearing traits that make cats such beloved companions.

Physical Characteristics:

Cats exhibit a wide range of physical features, which vary across different breeds. On average, adult domestic cats weigh between 4 to 5 kilograms (8.8 to 11 pounds) and stand about 23 to 25 centimeters (9 to 10 inches) tall at the shoulder. Their flexible bodies are supported by a skeletal structure that enables exceptional agility and stealthy movements. Cats possess sharp retractable claws that they use for climbing, hunting, and self-defense.

One of the most striking features of cats is their unique coat patterns and colors. From the sleek and solid-colored coats of breeds like the Bombay to the intricate tabby patterns seen in the Maine Coon, the feline world offers a diverse palette of fur variations. Additionally, some cats, like the Siamese, exhibit striking blue eyes that add to their allure.

Behavior and Communication:

Cats are known for their independent and solitary nature, but they also form deep bonds with their human caregivers. They are crepuscular animals, meaning they are most active during dawn and dusk. Cats are skilled hunters and possess excellent senses, including acute hearing and night vision. Their sharp retractable claws allow them to climb trees effortlessly, while their powerful hind legs provide remarkable jumping abilities.

Communication among cats and humans occurs through a combination of vocalizations, body language, and scent marking. Cats use various vocal cues, such as purring, meowing, hissing, and growling, to convey their needs and emotions. Body language, including tail movements, ear positioning, and facial expressions, plays a crucial role in feline communication. Scent marking, through rubbing or scratching, helps cats establish territories and communicate with other cats.

Health and Care:

Proper care is essential for ensuring the well-being of our feline friends. Cats require a balanced diet that meets their nutritional needs, with a focus on high-quality protein sources. Regular veterinary check-ups, vaccinations, and preventive treatments for parasites are crucial for maintaining their health.

Cats are highly self-grooming animals, spending a significant portion of their waking hours grooming their fur. However, occasional brushing can help prevent hairballs and keep their coats in good condition. Providing a safe and stimulating environment, including scratching posts, toys, and vertical spaces for climbing, helps fulfill their natural instincts.

Human Interaction and Cultural Significance:

Cats have a long and storied history intertwined with human civilizations. They were revered and worshipped in ancient Egyptian society, where they held sacred status as symbols of grace and protection. Today, cats continue to occupy a special place in our lives as beloved pets. Their playful antics, companionship, and ability to provide emotional support have made them cherished members of countless households worldwide.

Conclusion:

From their elegant physical attributes to their distinct behaviors and captivating personalities, cats have secured a special place in our hearts. Whether curled up on our laps or playfully chasing toys, these enchanting creatures bring joy and companionship to our lives. Through their independent spirit and enduring charm, cats have woven themselves into the fabric of human culture, leaving an indelible mark on our shared history.